MW01250548

THE
FLAME
TREE

THE
FLAME
TREE

CLARISE
FOSTER

© 1998, Clarise Foster

All rights reserved. No part of this book may be reproduced, stored in a retrieval system or transmitted in any form or by any means without written permission from The Muses' Company, an imprint of J. Gordon Shillingford Publishing Inc., except for brief excerpts used in critical reviews.

The Muses' Company Series Editor: Catherine Hunter
Cover design by Terry Gallagher/Doowah Design Inc.
Author photo by Karen Barry
Printed and bound in Canada

Published with the assistance of the Manitoba Arts Council and The Canada Council for the Arts.

Canadian Cataloguing in Publication Data

Foster, Clarise, 1955–
    The flame tree

ISBN 1-896239-39-0

    I. Title.

PS8561.O7742F53 1998 C811'.54 C98-900953-X
PR9199.3.F68F53 1998

For My Brother:
Shawn Michael Foster
1958–1990

CONTENTS

THE POEM GETS A NAME

WHEN I HAVE NOT SLEPT

IF I LOOK

LEGEND OF TWO LOVERS' LEAP

On Guam there is a legend that once, long ago, the chief of a small village promised his beautiful young daughter in marriage to the Captain of a Spanish ship. The daughter, who was in love with a young man from her own village, refused to marry the Spanish Captain. Instead, that night she ran away with her lover. It it said the Spanish Captain was furious and pursued her to the place now called Two Lovers' Leap. There the young woman and the young man were surrounded by the Captain's contingent of soldiers. Still the young woman refused. Rather than marry this man she had no feelings for, she tied her hair to the hair of her lover and together they jumped from the great height of the cliff into the sea. Their bodies were never found.

—Guam legend

if i look

the road to two lovers' leap
is paved now
but the boonies are still thick
on either side
with walking trees & tangantangan
too much green flesh
it hurts my eyes
the odd hibiscus
a bloody wound
the war still here
if i look
in the bright clearing
of cliff and sky
too many tourists
bus loads
each one a fine line
written against the ocean precipice
with the sadness of old men
their faces thin and dry
in the luminous wake
of young children
stumbling up
through the past
their limbs
fluid with sunlight

so much has changed here
yet stayed still
as time will lift all things
& set them down again
with the difference of tears

it has been so many years i say
& now where will i begin

bombs

on guam there were bombs left over from the war i imagined
they were buried & hidden & just sitting around in back yards
under palm trees because the teachers as we sat squirming on the
shiny wood gym floor our shoes & sweaty bare legs squeaking
showed us photographs black & white & tacked on to big boards
too small to see back where i was of bombs different sizes &
shapes & of children scarred who played with them accidentally
& told us bombs could if we held them or picked them up blow
our hands off or burn us & lani & maria & becky & me we were
too scared to go up to look but the boys did sniffing on stiff legs
hands jammed tight into pants pockets oohing & awing & want-
ing to find one & we thought we wouldn't find any if we didn't
look & if we did we would run away screaming to tell our
mothers but we'd never touch one so we didn't go up to see
what they looked like & now i wish i had because maybe then i
would have seen the ones that lodge big & metallic in the gut &
explode & shatter & singe inside like him leaving like you dying

rosa maria magdalene

rosa maria magdalene you have waited
for such a long time under the flame tree
in the sweet island heat waiting weak
with your trembling this delicate leaf
your brown face barely seen for the
emerald sparkle of green the tendrilous
hands of bougainvillea spilling into
the breeze white and purple and pink
this fragrant tangle of leaves festooned
with the laughter of small children
their bodies dangled into heat as ripe
as the diamond sleeve of ocean you can
see this brilliant fire of blue beyond the red
earth at your feet beyond the sleepy
curve of the street where you watch
your hard eyes burning into hot sun
your sadness born of the sea the ancient
bones of lovers you have grieved into
sunsets waiting for me with the broken
bead of your heart the woman you would
meet who bleeds into the dark an àngry
river of scars my arms marked you said
with the beauty of stars remembering
the open wound of your chest spoken
into my pale flesh this small spark like
the flaming heart of the tree where you
wait now across oceans with the body of
your grief this frail light barely visible
in the bright shimmer of leaves

dededo

today we are looking for our past
everything overgrown
with concrete glass & roads
the village we once lived in
like any other suburb
back home in winnipeg

except for the endless scatter of chickens
the boonie dogs that roam
though piles of garbage

& the plumeria trees
there are not many here anymore
the hard green of hibiscus
grown now mostly in pots
& when we find the house
we're not sure
it was ever really ours

but i know somewhere
there is a photograph of me
on that very porch
taken when i was fourteen
about the same age
as the young girl who leans now
almost exactly where i stood
but there is no smile
just a girl of fourteen
her face a puzzle
& her skin the cool shade of teak

so many memories
of this house
how the tin roof leaked
in the room
where my sister & i slept

when storms rattled
the thick branches
of the mango tree outside
small green fruit hammered
the metal over our heads like fists

but mostly i remember
how pale i was
in that pink dress
& those white shoes
a weary smile
bitten into my face
holding on
to the school books
under my arms as if
they were huge stones
a fourteen year old girl
shouldn't look so tired
bent with her own weight
as a walking tree is bent
in the struggle to free
its long powerful roots
from the red island earth

& although
the photo is long lost
it is how i will
always remember myself
fourteen & crooked

watching my reflection
in the car window
as it frames
the lovely young
girl on the porch

suddenly glad
for the way the past
overtakes us
fills the spaces we
leave behind

truth

as if he were talking about
a bestseller or perhaps a magazine
my father says the bible
is a good read
& i say
i am afraid of flying
not in the same breath
but it's the way we talk
my father & i
talk & don't listen
because there's more
to fear than we think
more than what glistens
in the empty mirror
of his face
& in mine
as we make
casual conversation
piece it together
from the usual bits
the world according to him

most of the time
there is no use arguing
neither of us
particularly faithful
to any one thing
though he says
he still believes in god
& i say
i believe in writing

all the same
i want to know
why he quit painting
but still afraid to ask

my father as easily angered
as i am confused
both of us with tempers
his more obvious than mine
as he leans back
in a white plastic lawn chair
the island night behind him
like his eyes changing as he speaks
from fiery orange to blue
& then dark

by midnight
we are both tired of our stories
especially the ones we don't tell

my father after school
in his small studio
the smell of oil
& turpentine
his thick fingers
rough with stain

once he told me
he figured he had
painted seven really
good paintings
in his life

sometimes i imagine
my father is disappointed
with himself with me
wonder if i should ask

my father reaches for his wineglass
in faint porch light
as i reach for mine
our silence
suddenly awkward

as if we haven't
had enough
this time
to get it right

the white stone circle
for my brother Shawn

and there was the time you chased me around the betel
nut tree in our front yard   with a dead toad   the stiff grass
under our bare feet like straw   and you hit me square
in the middle of my back   the thud sickening   your smile
sticking in my mind as i chased you back   around and
around   your laughter spinning above my head
in thick wet air

and the time you came running into the house your face pale and
your eyes full of tears   saying you were cursed because of the
circle   the white stone circle you and Roake found   stepped into
the ring   and the scary old woman who caught you and told you
that a circle of small stones was home to fairies and spirits   that
those who stepped into the circle would die young and our
mother said this wasn't true   just superstition   wiped your eyes
said   her eyes not sure   you could never die from a circle   not
like that and you didn't
just then

and there was the time we drove dad's old honda around
the house without his permission   the engine sucking
wheels spinning   our laughter   echoed   loud against the
afternoon   i remember how we thought we were so cool
your elbow crooked out of the window into the hot sun
the smell of you as we sweated and bounced
in the heat of our defiance   the smell of a young boy
all toads and grass

but did you forget or remember when death came circling
in on you   still young after all those years   the last gasp
of breath taking you back to your birth   and perhaps before
memory   this ring of fire closing behind your eyes   the place
in your back   where the toad hits first   the sickening thud
of stone   of your heart turning white with fear
death weighing you down into the mouth of the cold
earth   a slight parting of lips pale
the grass wet with tears

the photo
for my mother

my mother shows me
a photograph
of a fruit stand
she took in bali
& i am surprised
delighted
by the way
it catches my eye
like a poem
i say

how it frames
the almost
evening air
against wood
like bone
& fruit
which does not glow
but darkens
into heavy
earthen tones
deep moss &
terracotta &
mustard gold

i can tell
my mother
thinks me
a bit crazy
but when i say
it's no joke
i'm serious
it startles
her too
because she says
she is pleased

as if she
actually believes me
this time

& in this
my mother
seems suddenly
very old as if
she will fold
any moment
into dust
or my arms

& for once
we almost
hold each other
across the separateness
of our lives
almost touch but don't
the way we rarely smile
in my father's photographs
where we are negatives
of ourselves
far from perfect

& so
when my mother asks
if i would like a copy
of her photograph
i say no
say it has
something
to do with perfection
how it fades
if you get too
close

night catch

with the last breath of sun
twilight perfectly tropical
riffles palm leaves
whispers at the reef's coral shore
where the lantern glow of sky
silhouettes the slow dance
of the fishermen
as they heave their nets
into the almost night
into flight   as if they were birds
the fine white knot of wings stretched
over ocean   over the liquid spines of fish
until there is no more sight left
in the warm air
to tell the difference

a fisherman's lamp
or a star

laundry

at the laundromat in yigo
my mother asks me about poetry
she actually uses the word
says she is proud
& i don't know
whether to laugh
or cry or just answer
for all the times
she has never asked
& so
i fold shirts

precisely
until my hands begin to ache
& when she asks a second time
even more politely
my cheeks burn
it is hot in here i say
as if i haven't heard
as if my mouth weren't
full of other words
some of them poems

but my mother is nothing
if not persistent
she says she really wants
to learn
that poetry scares her
& i see now
that i frighten her too
my mother suddenly
very small
her eyes crystal blue
when i tell her
this is who i am

tails

if you pull the tail off a gecko
it will wriggle like a blind worm
in the palm of your hand
on guam a blind worm is really a snake
but a tail is a tail
wriggling
even in paradise

an amputation of thought

how could you pull the tail off
how could you hold it to pull the tail off
how could you even think of it

it was she says an accident
the body escaping intact
the tail will grow back she says
hiding her cruelty behind tears
behind the fact it will grow back

she saw a gecko once with two tails
one growing out of the other
and she asks what does this mean

the tail repeating itself
which one is real
and does it matter
given two chances to survive
one tail lost in a fight

would it grow back twice
or get caught in a door
some have died this way
accidentally
their soft skin peeling
back along the spine
their eyes dried
into crisp black seeds

she remembers the eyes

one thing growing
out of the other
which one is real
and does it matter
in the absence
of chance

truth caught
in the smallness of a hand
the space of it smashed
until nothing is left

remembering
each time she hears
the door slam
to shut her eyes

waiting for the green flash

my father writes
but he doesn't write to me
he says it's a perfectly manly thing
says his father didn't write to him
even when he was overseas
fighting for his life he says
not my father then
just a boy of eighteen
a boy he says
meaning it to move me
& it does

because i lean toward him
knowing we are closer
in some inexplicable way
my father doesn't say
whether he wrote to his father
& i don't ask
just wonder if my grandfather
wrote like me
like my father
who has had too much to drink
though i'm not supposed to say
such things

we are here to watch the sunset
after fifteen years
my father & mother & me
in this hotel bar
waiting for the green flash
& it comes & it goes
my mother takes a picture
& i take a picture of her
my father orders another
dry martini on the rocks
he says *please*
his voice almost pleasant
& his smile a boyish flash of teeth

a pose i think
but i have no film left
no idea what he means
except that i should lean
bend closer when he speaks
& say nothing

guam island highway

today
i am tired of remembering
all i want to do
is drink coffee
read my book
but there is so much
they say
i haven't seen yet
so much that has changed
& so today
we drive

meander
past the university
& **talofofo**
inarajan
umatac
melisso
all the villages
i remember
& the road still the same
still dangerous when it rains
my mother says
as she drives her car slowly
against the winding of it
because you never know

& it's true
today the clouds are low
as we make our way
along the coast
which has not changed
although it has grown
yacht clubs and hotels

she takes me to **ga'an**
where the water they say
ran red during the war
red with the blood
of those never young here
& those born of this place
never to grow old

the ocean peaceful now
bunkers & guns
vague reminders
memories i don't own
come rushing back to me here
so old sometimes
older than the sea
& the sky

or is it only the sound
of my own ancient heart
the rush of blood
in my ears
that i hear in the wake
of so many voices

this island's past
like a road that winds itself
twists past all that is memory
what is left here
for me

on the way back
we pass a carabao
with her young calf
resting too close
to the road

as we continue to drive
it occurs to me

it is
raining

leaving home

crying for two days straight
in a honolulu hotel after i
left home for the first time
i thought i would die wanting
you so bad to want me back
not here not cut in half
in this strange room full
of tears crying an ocean too vast
to see you on the other side dry
eyed with your sweet plumeria
leis your one more glass of wine
to remember why i had to leave
this time for my own sake not
your peace of mind the ocean
calm and vast outside my hotel
room window tears under glass
flash unbroken in bright sunlight
knowing you wouldn't write
somehow knowing i'd survive
or die trying

learn to walk on water
the point of no return

WITHOUT A TRACE

THE WHITE LADY

Once long ago there was a young man who fell in love and wanted to marry a beautiful taotaomo'na, or spirit, who lived with her cousins in the jungle. When he proposed to taotaomo'na, who appeared to him in the form of a lovely young woman, she accepted. When the young man informed his parents of his intentions, they were outraged. His mother and father forbade the marriage, and when the young man persisted, his mother killed him. It is said his betrothed still waits for her dead lover at the Maina Bridge. She appears resplendent in white, and has long black hair that reaches down her back to the ground. Her presence is foretold by the scent of ilangilang, or flowering fadang. In other parts of Guam she smells of fresh wild lemon.

—Guam legend

how i remember you
for s.

when the deft wound
of dawn leaves sorrow
holding only one of us

i know by the mark
dreaming has left
on my skin
you are not fully gone
but winged in the way
summer is winged
with shadow

sometimes wind
reminds me
of the way water
bends everything
back into itself

a fact of blood
a fact of flight

butterflies

the way the old story goes
long ago in china there was a man
who dreamt he was a butterfly
awakened to find he might be
a butterfly dreaming he was a man
confused perhaps for a moment
he knew he was one or the other
but he thought one could be the other
and this he called
the transformation of things

calling out from his sleep *butterfly*
in the language i could speak once
having studied chinese
so long ago

remembering the word *hú dié*
and how i was afraid to say it
afraid i would make a mistake
saying something i shouldn't say
something that would give me away
all wings and dust this dream hidden
beneath the tongue remembering
between teeth clenched speaking only blood
into the dark throated crust
of my insect body

for i am the woman who sleeps
in the dream of butterflies
attempting chinese
into the open mouth of the sky
into the leaves of the black rooted tree
which does not answer flight
even to the trick of wings
to the language that will not sing
from my lips the dance of it

just before the tip the pin twisting
into the pit of my stomach

hú dié zaì hua cóng zhong fei wu
butterflies fluttered about the flowers

dream 1

i am looking for my mother
who is looking for me over
and over until i find her
a woman swept vaguely out
to sea reading a book no
a magazine she is smiling but
it is so far away i don't think
she can see me see what i have
to say so i wade thinking
i might make it as the ocean
turns to sand so fast i am
sinking but she grabs my hand
pulls me up and says *so what
do you have to say for your
self* and my mouth so full
of words spews nothing but glass
bits of teeth blood dribble spit
uterus got your tongue she says
watching my surprise *what did
you expect miracles* there are
tears in her eyes she says **this
is your dream** and goes back to
reading her magazine
upside down

the empty space

how a word is pondered
turned over on the tongue

to find the underside
the word that snakes
up through darkness

the word that crawls
into the dream
from a hole in the floor

from nothing
up into day
the word hissing

not a word at all
but the sound
of lips parting
the empty space
between a hand
and a face
whispering

   i love you

into your smallness
and how it
tastes

   not love at all

paper swans

it is hiroshima & i am thirteen
& there is a statue in the park
that flutters with thousands
of folded paper birds
origami i am told
but i am not listening
watching the silver paper
in the sun
thinking of the chain
i made once of gum wrappers
the museum behind us
full of keloid flesh in jars
like dead jelly fish
pictures & clothing
of the people burned
when the bomb was dropped

it is still hiroshima & i am still thirteen
& there is the night i dream
a thousand wings unfolding
red & black & silver
against an afternoon sky
not made of paper
jelly fish peel away with my hair
& i am thirsty my bones melting
& then there is nothing
but death wandering
with my eyes in hands folded neatly
as paper swans flutter
thousands of them
from a statue in the park

the dance
for Di

ah, dancer, ah, sweet dancer!
how you move
through that grey eyed
morning in june
to the furious beat of rain
on the cabin's thin roof
your body made to that tune
moving as if you had been born to it
the trees and the loons shimmering
with all their bright sadness
in the waking gloom
beyond the pale of windows

beyond the warmth of the room
where you dance to the rain
with your cups and your spoons
taking one step too soon
sending everything crashing
the kitchen strewn
with sharp bits of glass
and the tears of your trembling
remembering perhaps
the leathered heel of a hand
or a mother's tight wrath
or worse
how i wanted to hold you
until the terror passed
but could not move

finding myself alone
in the room of my mother's eyes
watching from a distance
the dance of a child
stumbling to the beat
with two left feet

like falling rain

sisters
for Tracy

sister   such a foreign word you occupy
so many rooms   my mind dwells
on the other life   rooms sealed years ago
the three of us   we had a brother then
only you & i now barely speaking two words

sisters rooms   we shared one once   the
two of us miles apart   so far it was hard
sometimes   two sisters long ago   we
could call   we never do   it is assumed
we are fine

sisters   our blood traced   in hearts   graves
we have buried ourselves bones   the closets
talk time   rattle in our throats   say something
will you call   missing us   our love   sister
we are missing

sister   you come from this name   that was long ago
in those rooms sealed in dust   in our dreams lost
the two of us think *too late maybe*   writing past
all this time gone   who could say anything
make us less distant

sisters apart miles   could we be any different
from each other i don't know   listen to the word
our tongues voices around it louder loudest on
his lips   he is dead now   only the two of us left

sister we occupy this word   you and i
say something

40

the way we are all tied

in memory of D.V.

on this windblown afternoon
my hands grab
through thick underbrush
& my feet stumble
stinging nettles jab
through my clothes
someone says
poison oak
but i don't know
what it looks like
& there's no time to ask

i am looking for you
& for what i don't want to find

what *missing*
means

either injured or
dead

the tall bush rustles
swallows bodies whole
spits them out again
in & out   out & in
we are fading fast
with the sunlight
& in my head now
i can hear your voice
sound but no words
like the whisper of leaves
i know you
& i don't know you
the line that separates you
from everything else
has become blurred

it makes no sense
if there is any sense in loss
that you would not be here

the whine of a siren pitches
hard against my ear
but i must keep looking
moving through the tangled
grass & setting sun
i can see only brilliance
for this moment
everything growing perfectly
the rocks & the trees & the grass
until the breeze lifts my name
& someone says
they have found you

but i can't imagine what that looks like
& i don't ask
on this windblown afternoon
my eyes burn through trees
without tears
my feet are stone

i am still
looking for you
the woman i remember
with a smile like
some bright august afternoon
& how we lost you
the way most of us lose
sight of ourselves
unable to see
what we cannot face

i wonder sometimes
if the wish for death
isn't a need to believe
as children believe
in the sanctity
of a place
what was it
we wanted from you

they say they found you
peaceful
the knot in your chest
grey
as the one
at your throat

afraid
to look now
in case i might find

no difference in the ways
we are tied

how an afternoon
can become
a very fine line
in the end

drawn
as each breath
is drawn
the same colour

as sky

it didn't bleed

last night in a dream   i put a wooden stake into   my head with a
hammer   as if i were some sort of vampire or crazy   but it didn't
bleed   and no one seemed to notice but me   when i couldn't
breathe at the foot of a long flight of stairs   every step a tooth   in
this big yawn of a house   bare except for the laughter of chairs
and two boys   one named tristan   young and very fair   the
way i remember my mother eating her hair   like pasta   at the
kitchen table   unable to care about what she thought was
strange anymore   and me watching her through the blue dust of
air   feeling my eyes sting   with the dream i still wear   when it is
morning   and a boy barely sixteen   if a day   opens the hard fist
of his face   to say   touch me   and i do   and my hand as it comes
away from his cheek   with a perfect ring   a wound   in my palm
bleeding

dream 2

tonight i am walking in grandma's garden
with an empty tobacco can around my neck
the string stained red

i am looking for raspberries
but find cabbages instead   rotting carrots
the roses are all dead   withered and strewn
some still dangling from the fence

after awhile
i decide this is useless
there is nothing left
not even the trees

but as i turn i discover her
my grandmother hiding
an old woman in the weeds
she is cutting up photographs
oblivious or so it seems
to her destruction

suddenly she begins to chase me
eyes straight ahead   flaring red
her kindness all spent whispered and dead
scissors flashing wildly

as she runs she thrusts out her wrists
gaping bloody mouths that spit and hiss
as madness pours rage thick
the colour of raspberries

to mark my hands   my face

mary mary quite contrary
how does your garden grow

grandmother smiling
as the darkness turns to stone

without a trace

i could waste away right here
trying to say what i have to say
smoke too many cigarettes   not eat
but then who cares anyway
he is already dead   perhaps so am i
sitting on this hard chair
trying to remember someone
i would rather forget
so very sick of seeing his face   his eyes
in the mirror of my computer screen
blue like the rest of us

the man of my grandmother's dreams
gone to seed too quickly
his beauty   the schemes
whisky bottles hidden in trees
the dirty clothes hamper
how he stared at me
so hard i couldn't think sometimes
wanted to run when he touched me

afraid

of the money he gave me
the way he would say
i was his favourite granddaughter
told me snakes crawled from cracks
in the kitchen floor

if there is more
i don't remember it

something inside torn
like the pages of a book
left open in the sun
the text which eventually fades
not even a trace

yet there is this heat
written into my bones
this wasting away

too logical to be a dream

this is about politics
not mothers
small men with their big machines
and trees the color of money
the BIG BUCK
stopping at the table where i sit
with my friend and a beer
and she says
if i had the guts i think i'd go
punk dye my hair green

i nod   light my cigarette   say
power comes from the barrel of a smoking gun
knowing this is the right thing to say
and she agrees

so what do you think of red ?

and the man they call crazy eddie
because he stinks   pees his pants
sits down right next to us and pretends to read
his arms stretched with nothing
in between dirty fingers
the silence screams

14 women murdered in montreal

and the waitress who is really just the radio
leans   whines into my ear
it's those bloody feminists
barely able to move
i say to my friend
there are mothers in this dream
can't you see?

and she says   *shocking*
pink ... blue

*what do **you** think ?*

THE POEM GETS A NAME

PROMISE

In the past, hilitai, or monitor lizards, were black and could sing. The hilitai was so proud of its beautiful voice, it could not resist showing off in front of all the other animals. The totot, or Rose Dove, jealous of the lizard's ability to sing, pointed out that while the hilitai had the most beautiful voice, its feathers were far more colourful than the lizard's blank skin. This in turn upset the hilitai who ran to its friend the ko'ko', the Guam rail, and asked the bird to paint him. The ko'ko' agreed on the condition that the lizard would paint him in return. So the ko'ko' painted little yellow dots all over the lizard. The hilitai was so impressed with the way he looked, he immediately wanted to show the other animals, but the ko'ko' reminded him of his promise. So the hilitai began to paint the bird, but desperate to show off, the lizard ran off before he had finished painting his friend. The ko'ko' was furious. The bird chased after the lizard, until he caught him, pecking him with his hard beak, and splitting the hilitai's tongue. This is why the monitor lizard is no longer able to sing, and the rail is striped only around the eye and on the stomach.

—Guam legend

not on trees

and no   poems don't grow on trees
although sometimes they taste
as sweet as ripe mango in the hot
sun all sticky and warm sweet juice
sparkling off your chin dribbling
down a child's dark arm easy
as laughter   as rain

no not trees   although sometimes
you can pick them out of the blue
in the pattern of a leaf out of
emerald afternoons woven
with pandanus and federico and
wild hibiscus hold ebu with its rare
translucence a moist jade
against your skin steal the
salamander's touch

not trees   although sometimes
you can climb one high enough to hear
the fragrant rush of your own voice like
wind singing so flushed with heat
and rust everything encrusted in this
place with the sea and fine coral dust
feel just this once the brilliant wave
of beach with its white sand gently
thrust like a bright tongue into your
mouth that comes undone with starfruit
the golden flesh of sun

and sometimes you can breathe
the o so green air like fire pull it into
your lungs until the heart is burned
to the almost edge of desire the bloody
spire of peaks turned now distant against
your cheek the distance you could reach
if only each word would fall as easily
as sleep or papaya shake this island
dream as you might a tree
to find your hands full

nocturn

(the poem gets a life)

the poem is slipping
away again
this time it slides
right out of the room
and across the street
into this little greasy spoon i know
where it sits alone on a stool
looking very cool
in my leather jacket
at the front counter
smoking cigarettes
and drinking black coffee

i can see from the window
it's pretending to be me
but when i try to follow
the door holds a knife to my cheek and says
the poem is not ready to leave   not yet
and the poem remains awfully silent
although now it looks frightened
as it lights another cigarette

later when the poem creeps back into my room
smelling vaguely of sex
cigarette smoke and booze
it smiles very sheepishly
and stumbles to offer me the moon
an offer i feel i can't refuse

but as i move to touch it
the moon comes loose
its light slipping through
the darkness like glass
how it stains the room
strangely the colour of
my hands writing blood

into the body of the poem
that has no tongue
the wound of it disappearing
into the dawn's early rust
becoming nothing more
than the poem in my side

a speck of dust
in the one good eye
that has been written

oracle
(the poem gets a name)

the poem has decided
to be my brother
the one who died of aids
and because i only had one
there can be no mistake
this is who the poem is
today

with its gaunt face
and swollen hands
when it says **save me**
and i can't
it doesn't take me long to know
the poem is going nowhere
making its way
through the broken teeth of my brain
to linger momentarily
a flicker in the luminous rage
which slips back
as quickly as it came
repeating the same hackneyed phrase
the words **i love you**
so commonly placed on pale lips
the mouth shedding kisses
like rain into the black corner
of the poem's abyss
the brother who sits empty
contemplating
the hollow bones of his wrists
an oracle licked by flame
to say just the poem's name

and then
        fade away
                again

addressing the poem
(to the poem)

so tell me the ways a heart grows cold

one hand pressed into breath
to feel the throat's emptiness
the slow turn of a spark
as the tick of flame
counts the heart
among the living
just below the thaw of skin

& if o poem
i put it to your lips again
would you say

> *count on greener pastures*
> *the way a cow numbers her days*
> *in grass*

without a stitch

there's something amiss in the way
the poem sits without a stitch
leaving nothing to the mind but
the sweet rhythm of skin assuming
it is most out of line for a poem to take
the time for a leisurely dip if you
catch its drift feeling its hips glide
along the cool surface of lips making
waves some would say as the ardent tongue
slips into the poem's wet abyss taking
what desire comes with the swift gift
of a kiss telling the fragrant swell
which lifts each rib to the burning
quick of fingers as the poem lingers
on the verge of shore knowing its body
more than a poem can possibly grasp
with the golden cord of its hands
unravelling like sand into the blue
flesh of sky

no longer blue

klee raced across the page and
dropped his pants where **picasso**
lost a stroke walking with **braque**
through the valley of stone they
were searching for the woman of
the rocks to tell them something
they might already know and **matisse**
painted bright orange and naked came
instead with a bowl of still life strapped
to his head his lions all dead and told
them nothing and grew very old and died
before the angel of **chagall** could save
him flying over and over again like
a dive bomber until it gave birth
to a child who drifted down to earth
and turned to dust before their feet
and from somewhere came a laugh
swirling green and blue and red
and purple that went mad under
the stars and strangled them into
cornflowers stuffed in a severed
ear melting into time propped up
in the desert next to the christ of ice
cubes turning colour in the sun
at which point **braque** ran away across
the ocean that was no longer blue
and disappeared and **picasso** feeling
his pecker rise traced in the sand what
he thought was a woman peeing because he
could no longer remember what either
looked like

looking back on kerouac

on the road again
eh jack
why don't you fly

tick tick tick

time as it dances
skipped generations
your cool boy
leaves nothing
of his hot glance
but sex

Sssssssssss.........

the first letter
of the beat
some one must coin
2 cents for words
and you speak
nothing of the
atrial

the squeezing of valves
of chests

the morning becomes
a red ghost careening
in its fast car

can fish turn
new leaves

does light have thumbs

you touch yourself
in the mirror
to find only the left
page only to be
left paging
yourself

Dr. Sax Dr. Sax

what reflection
won't cure
death like
some windup toy

smoking
marijuana
behind the
pool hall

you are caught
making heroes
out of dust

all this swagger
the buzz
the dark
smile stumbles

true

somewhere
at the mouth
we are all criminals

our nerves swallowed
by the fickle drug
of grief

yours dreaming
at the speed of words
another empty fix

dreaming of your sweet jail boy
all cock and spit
as he drives bare
chested

slips

speeding through
the golden
needle of your skin
eyes hooked
to the disappearing
point of night

the day's mindscape
a hollow place for
stars and breath
looking for my own heart
among the stones
i will find a wing

its range of motion
full circle

click click click

against the shoulder
the neck
in its blind socket
ricocheting back
across startled
generations

polka deaf

treble clef burns
my hand slipping
can't play no jazz man
cool water o
can't start any riffs
throat ain't sticking
no thread tune
so many strings corded
rope time tap gold
heel moments slide
get no dance band
sittin   old   old
water cold polka deaf
waltz reason
        and
skin hard
fingers callous
meaning lips
let half notes
be written
mine blue jive step
can't christen
no bone night
moon sliver wrist

bend   touch   sky

WHEN I HAVE NOT SLEPT

CREATION

"...in the beginning, in the limitless space of the Universe, before the creation of the earth and the sky there lived an omnipotent being named Putan. As time passed Putan felt himself about to die, so he called his sister Fu'una, who, like himself, had been born without the help of father or mother, and gave her explicit instructions as to the disposal of his body, and conferred upon her all his miraculous powers. He decreed that upon his death his eyes should become the sun and the moon; his breast the sky; his back the earth; his eyebrows the rainbow and the rest of his anatomical parts, the lesser things of the world and the nether regions. In time Putan died, and Fu'una carried out her brother's wishes, and so the world was created."

—Chamorro myth

the gravity of light

Each time we make a choice, we pay
With courage to behold resistless day
And count it fair.
   —Amelia Earhart

& at what price
do you imagine fear
afraid for the moment
you will finally stumble
the courage it will cost
prepared for this
most if not all your life
& still surprised
when the day comes
to resist you

finding as you pour
over the bright instrument
of your hands everything
in its opposite
& the ocean
as you stumble
wave after wave
never so abstract
as you discover terror
to be endless as the sky
your daring
as the moment falters
so divinely shaken
but the only moment
you have

so go ahead
invoke your strange god
strike a barter
with your tongue
prop your mouth
with words

your voice as it spills
a brilliant interstice
blue everywhere you look
& the silence
as it opens beyond
into a darkness empty
as you have always known
the moon to be a question
luminous as your soul

the panic then
when all you ever wanted
was to touch
the sky

& now that
you are falling
the wind in your chest
so impossibly silver
you would offer
wings & prayers
taste abandon
utter palms
as they might
sink or swim
the nights more glorious
for the risk you have taken
it is only fair

what you wouldn't give
in this fiercest of flights
suspended as you are
helpless before imagination
before the gravity of light

that you were able
to embrace
the uncertainty of distance
tell from a sweeter height
the bitter slake of stars

counting madness
among your maps
where fire leads
& thirst defines you
every moment a mirror
in which you imagine yourself
to be lost & the days
reflection so vivid
you would ask
anything in exchange
for the long arm of sun
this breath of heat
paradise riding
on your crooked heart
& your heart
as it beats
a desert pulse
of dreams & blood

corners

my cat chews
at the corners of my books
the slimmest volumes of poetry first
her mouth still too small
for the fat loam of fiction
clawing at whatever i read
until i must abandon this too
as i have left so many places

understanding as light fills
an empty room
that even islands
can be corners
bland with brilliance
& frayed
where the sun has bitten
land from water
where a slow wind shakes
evening gently to the bone
& ocean swallows
even the resilient fire
of flame trees
night left
with no other memory
but stars

my cat completely black
except for a white corner
of her stomach
a star perhaps
or the moon
& the ocean rising
each tide as it trembles
toward the reef & back
blue days torn as if by teeth
& sand

paradise wearing
thinnest at the corner
where sea is only deep
& dark waves
like the pounding of a heart

somewhere else
a carabao in an empty field
where an old man
plows his edge of the red earth
he knows silence
is the beginning
& this island
ends in that place
where there are no birds

the dark green foliage
of the banyans & the d'oak trees
inhabited now
by wind & snakes
as snake remembers only
snake

this place we called nowhere
finding ourselves
on the middle of a huge map
& then finding ourselves
lost again

the cat is never lost
she rides
my shoulder
down the stairs
& back again
past the room
she has strewn
with my papers
at the corner
of each page
she has left
her mark

there are times
when i have no idea
where i have
been except for
what slips
from my fingers
sometimes
it is a book
with bite marks
in the corner

& sometimes
it is just a corner

a place
where the light fills
evening with so much sand
i can't think
wondering if my cat
will remember me
the island i leave
no bigger than a shadow

my absence that small

grey

1.

she knows
grey as the colour of his leaving
his lips his hair his eyes his bones
now ashes   dust
ashes   dust
dust to dust

ashes

his smoke remnant of flame
licked up by the wind
transported
with the ease
of a stiff winged bird
back   back to the beginning

grey
nothing
grey

not like all those days
hospital rooms
melting
one into the other
the urgent not wanting
& knowing
so fucking scared

his skull drilled
his vomit stinking
his hair falling out   in clumps

no   not like that
she believes

not like that

2.

she sits with the greyness
that is her brother
sunlight forced through small windows
the scent of flowers in pots & bowls & vases
with the sound of wind chimes tossed
gently by the wind outside

the red cloisinne urn
she thinks
too small to hold
all that remains

her own heart dust
she is calm
she believes she understands

later twilight settles
her face empty
as calm disappears

3.

slowly darkness veils stillborn light
the air is thick & cool
her father makes the engine hum
the night's ride smooth & fast
& her brother is sleeping

his hands finally quiet
& he is sleeping

his body bent soft
& he is sleeping

his head slightly tilted
& he is sleeping

& he is sleeping

      he is   sleeping

sleeping
                                                                                      &

he
he   sleeping

is

is   he sleeping

no she says

no

4.

she takes the necklace from the open drawer
the necklace he was wearing when
the necklace she gave him
gold

gold the colour
of absence
she thinks
grief
in the absence
of anything else
tangible
the absence
in which
she fingers
the metal
of her own pulse
the absence in which
she discovers loss
a vague calligraphy
silence does not
seem to understand

5.

& gold the colour
of waiting
the colour of her
still waiting
in the four white
walls of a moment
where there is no time
where the brother
she does not know
has become
another distance
the distance blood
becomes

the past
between them
burning so arduous
& so wide
afraid she will never
make it to the other
side that she
will drown
under the burden
of her own shadow
waiting
with the long passage
of sunlight until
she is too late even
to save her own
reflection

waiting
until she sees
her brother
at the end of a long
blue tunnel

realizing
the cold currency
he has spent

a necklace not enough
nor love

6.

somewhere there is music
it is a dream
where each moment is a voice
time ticking in a thousand desperate glances
& the slow ghost of a crowd
she cannot tell from sleep

everything dancing

& the dream where her brother's
eyes turn first blue &
then dark

unable to find the floor
for all the feet
the night has grown
extra legs a forest of empty
moons blind as trees
where hands
in still life
keep reaching

& time
continues to dance
without sound
the hole in memory
a heart leaves
when it is gone
& the heart
she finds
in the first break
of morning
her chest seized
legs pumping
past cars past parks

past white houses & red houses
past houses the colour of doors
past memory past dreaming past
the place the road gives out
that sharp edge over oceans

where she heaves the smallness
of her brother's name

& the greyness
that answers

silence fills
the march air

the swimmer

after one of the swimmer series by visual artist Betty Goodwin

the gash at her heel
luminous as sun
dripping in an old sky
the furious liquid
beneath the thin skin
she wears a membranous
sorrow not scars
& the wrist where the past
finds her swimming in place
every place viscous
with sleep or darker

in better light
you would see
her jaw working
in painted light
so little of her face appears
the way an ocean appears
to be calm

yes she thinks
or you imagine
truth as it lies
in understatement
the elongated
understatement of her bones
as she pulls herself
toward the blue of surface any surface
the two halves of her world
held together with pieces of tape

already
she has no pulse
but still she swims
because swimming
is all she is

her elegance

drawing her
through the needle
does not
elaborate her eyes
but with desperate scrutiny
line falls away from line
until there is only
the vagueness of colour
finding in her eyes
the torpor of rust
although the memory
behind them remains
urgently tropical
her mind tethered
as palms are tethered
to the sure velvet
of a white sand beach

she knows to sink
she must remember
but her eyes are drawn
however simply
straight ahead

each line becomes
a movement she must forget
forgetting there is a forgiveness in this
& beyond the blank edge of
the painting a wound

& the painting where she still swims   deeper
for the water has gone hard
with shape & summers
sometimes you want to imagine
her head or the stray sketch of her arm
as it slightly bruises the surface
but essentially she remains the same
essentially suspended
the sun as it opens at her ankle

& the sun as it is balanced
between two surfaces of light

the light above   the light below

when i have not slept

morning trees
brittle with winter
shake stone from
shallow limbs
this not a sound
but a silence
i have heard
in breathing
the dull silver
of grace
stiff as bone
listening
when i cannot sleep
to the indifferent prowl
of snowfall

strange
but whatever
animal the night
becomes
it is the dark
bereft in me
that recalls dawn
fallow eyes lifted
to the small music
of shadows blooming
listless flowers
to the sun's frozen heat
waking then
when i have not slept
to the unfurling
of your absence
like the snow outside
longing spilled
into every scintillant
corner of breath
dawn when absence
is not a colour

but the distance
between heart
& words

blue as it is a much harsher light
blue before darkness
blue of eyes
blue that is borrowed
words that are also blue
cobalt, turquoise
blue that is love
blue that is not
the blue that is the measure
of waiting

& light as it begins here
where the sky is cracked
the moon beneath it
pale as flesh or grief
the morning's blue
when the feather of
pulse is cut
& the wing scatters

sometimes
the air's early stillness
frightens me
as does the bitter
shrieking of crows
even in deepest winter
their hearts not stopped
their blood too ancient
eyes black as sleep

& sometimes
it is you
who frightens me
the sorrow you bear
like the sorrow
that bears winter
in its deepest heart
your eyes older

than the stones you leave
despairing over
the tenuousness
of your gifts
never quite sure
whether you are real
or figment
& sometimes
the night
so deftly parched
you appear
as easily
as you disappear

i think of you often
as i think of the tree
that shapes a burnt horizon
finding in every grain of sand
a desert you complete
as if thirst were
the only light
& in this incandescence
bones
as far as touch
vision

remember
the skeletal bird
as it rose from
your hand like a
phoenix it is true
you have been
transformed
in the end never
what you say
but what you mean
& every word the sun setting
in you its death curved
meticulous into some
dark ornithic soul

or is it morning that
travels through your
arced limbs so brilliant
& so pink
that blue becomes
the contradiction

my own bones piled neatly
across the shallow
arm of winter
a cairn of spaces
in memory of your eyes
while the trees
crooked with silence
shake dawn
from brittle fingers
the morning sky
falling then
in terse stones
against my windows
first blue flecked with
brown & then brown with red

the wind outside has become
an uncertain homage
as if your absence
were suddenly
burned into my skin
& i can feel you
one breath at a time
your cheek smooth
against my face
lifting my heart
gently as you
would a stone
afraid for the mark
you leave not a scar
but an opening
where the moon
still shivers full

listening as i might
for the distant shriek of crows
when all i wish for
is the simple sound
of your footsteps
knowing silver
not a silence
but the grace with
which a cloud moves
across an empty sky
even in winter

the blue that finds
you missing
& the light
that brings
you home

the clarity of winter

tonight i can see
the bright bones
of the moon
it is that close
counting on my
own proximity
the nearness
of something
other than skin
to protect me
from the ghosts
of the stars outside
the small fire of the river
i remember
the blur of crossing
in so much heat

& the clarity of winter now
as i drive
the fullness of the moon
reminding me
of the last bird
as it turned
in the candle eye
of a snake
the liquid filigree
of its tiny skeleton
barely visible
as i am barely visible
against the black
of the sky
in its pale shell

wanting to drive faster
toward some invisible
point of memory
break from the blindness
that holds me forever

fixed to the vision
i was born with

but there is a limit
even to speed
& there is night
that unchangeable distance
no matter how fast or hard i drive
i can never shorten it
i will never be further away

death is like this
& light

how ever close i come
there is always the past
to slow me down
measure one place
from another

it is the distance
between the sharp edge
of a knife & skin
it is the feeling
of being always
in a movie

knowing what will
happen
& at the same time
helpless

what summer was it
or was it even summer at all
in that island place
of only two seasons
either wet or dry
cold would have to wait
at least five more years
but by then

i was already gone
& you were leaving

funny how
neither of us
went back
not really

funny in the way
mangoes smell as they rot
in the hot sun
memory that pungent

i remember the smell of the sea that day
the way the cave smelled
the time it took to get there

the way i remember
sunlight pouring
through the small embrasure
in the cave's far wall
& you barely able to reach
the undivided tenderness

with which our father lifted you
forgotten as each of us
took a turn at playing soldier
pointing fingers
out at the banyan trees
the ocean far below

this cave a hospital
during the war
we imagined
like the war
we pretended
with neighbourhood kids
where the injured
were always safe
& a hospital
even a hospital
in a cave like a church
somehow sacred

no idea
how easy it becomes
to make enemies
no idea how easily
pleasure comes undone

only our laughter
echoing ripe
as gunshots
as we hunted
for something
to make us bigger

how far i wonder
did we go
how far
& how strange
it felt then
to dig through
the debris
of our own shadows
later impossible
to wash the dark
from our hands

when i think of caves now
i think of something
slipping from its skin
& you at the mouth of it
a human shin bone
in your hand

i can't remember what you said
but i remember
the size of your voice
so much older

i had never noticed
the disappointment
in your eyes before

the years between us
never simple after that

the day after you died
i burnt my hand
the need perhaps to feel
something other than grief

it wasn't the first time
& it wouldn't be the last

pain as a kind of logic
you inflict upon yourself
when there are no other maps
no other ways to gauge distance

tomorrow morning
there will be nothing
left of the moon
but a scar

ACKNOWLEDGEMENTS

Some of these poems have appeared previously in *Praire Fire* and *Contemporary Verse 2*. The title *Sweet Dancer* is from a poem by W.B. Yeats of the same name published in the *Collected Poems of W.B. Yeats* (London: Macmillan, 1973). The translation of the last line in *Butterflies* was done with the help of *The Pinyin Chinese-English Dictionary* (Beijing: John Wiley and Sons). *The Legend of Two Lovers' Leap* is my own retelling of this story from memory. The Chamorro creation myth is taken from *Daughter of the Island: Contemporary Chamorro Women Organizers on Guam*, Second Edition, edited by Laura Marie Torres Souder (Latham: Micronesian Area Reasearch Center at the University of Guam, 1992). The White Lady and the monitor lizard legend are both from memory, informed by *Ancient Chamorro Society* by Lawrence J. Cunningham (Honolulu: Bess Press).

I would like to thank Catherine Hunter for her generosity as an editor, both for asking for this manuscript and for her firm but gentle encouragement in getting it ready for publication.

I would like to thank the Manitoba Arts Council for the financial support to complete the original draft of this manuscript. I would also like to thank Di Brandt for her assistance with earlier versions of this manuscript; Bernia Brandsteadter for her years of love and support in the writing of it; my oldest friend Cindy Mains for believing in me; as well as the members of my writing group, Susan Rempel-Letkemann, Rae Harris, Joan Thomas, Heidi Harms, Erika Ens, Melody Goetz, and Mirth Rosser for many evenings of laughter, good food and invaluable criticism.

Last, but never least, I would like to thank Susan for the gift she has made to me of her love of light, poetry and her infinite grace as a friend all of which continue to inspire me beyond words.

AFTERWORD

It is important to explain I was not born on Guam, but lived there for many years when my father took a teaching position on the island in 1969. Several poems in this collection have their origin in that experience. Guam remains an important place for me, and it is the context for a number of the memories I have of my brother, who died of AIDS in 1990, and to whom this book is dedicated.

Guam or "Guhan," which means "we have" in Chamorro, the indigenous language and culture, is 32 miles long, 9 miles at its widest point and 4 miles at its narrowest. A part of the Marianas Island chain, it is located in the South Pacific, closer to the Philippines and Japan than it is to Hawaii, its closest U.S. neighbour. Guam was 'discovered' in 1521 by Ferdinand Magellen, and has been subjected to outside political rule ever since, serving as a strategic military outpost for Spain, the United States, and Japan. Today it is a U.S. territory.

Chamorros are the aboriginal people of Guam. It is not known exactly where they orginated, although there is strong evidence to suggest they were of Southeast Asian descent. Today there are no full-blooded Chamorros left. Years of foreign occupation and inter-marriage have lead to the near extinction of both their ancient culture and ethnic heritage. In recent years there have been extensive efforts by Guamanians of Chamorro descent to preserve and reclaim their rich and colourful past.

During the Second World War, Guam was occupied by the Japanese from December 8, 1941 to July 27, 1944. Living conditions on the island during that time were unspeakable, with people forced to endure "atrocities, such as rape, torture, and even death, enforced manual labour and inhuman treatment in concentration camps." The battle by American armed forces to regain Guam from the Japanese was costly. In the end most of the island was levelled. People familiar with the primary battles of the Pacific campaign during WWII are more likely to be familiar with Saipan, also located in the Marianas Islands. Saipan is also thought to be where American aviator Amelia Earhart was imprisoned and eventually executed.

Today, Guam is a tourist mecca for Japan and the rest of Asia, and has more than its share of tacky souvenir shops, video arcades, restaurants and posh hotels. Its economy, long dependent on the U.S. military, has suffered with the recent downsizing of U.S. military installations. As a result, Guam has been forced to rely more on tourism. With the current economic climate in Asia this has been difficult.

In terms of the natural ecology of the island there have been ongoing problems with the environment. Currently one of the most pressing problems is the Philippine rat snake. Years ago, when machinery was being transported to Guam from the Philippines, Philippine rat snakes somehow managed to slip into the packing crates. Since then the rat snake, also known as the chicken snake, has proliferated to the extent that the birds once native to the island are now on the verge of extinction. The snakes hunt a variety of small prey, mostly at night, including the eggs of the Guam Rail, a small land bird found only on Guam.

Guam, in my experience, is a rather obscure location for most people, a place many people know of but know nothing about. These days, Guam to many North Americans is a distant place they read of in the newspapers, a place made notable by disaster— typhoons, earthquakes, and most recently a tragic plane crash. Guam in fact is a beautiful tropical island, lush all year round with banyan trees, coconut trees and, yes, flame trees. It is a place pristine with red hills and white sand beaches, where there are flowers beyond imagination and sea and sky so blue it seems impossible that blue could be any other colour. In short it is the paradise most of us dream of.

Guam's history is not immediately apparent from the long stretches of its beautiful beaches. Construction and the relentless tangle of vegetation have overtaken many of the most painful reminders of its past. But if you look, it is there. Some of the old Spanish buildings remain. Monuments built to chronicle the feats of ancient Chamorro heroes and modern-day soldiers alike are found as you travel the old Island Highway. Offerings of cigarettes, flowers and trinkets are still routinely left by visitors at the sites of strategic battles and memorials to the war dead. Many large guns, bunkers and caves have been preserved to commemorate the liberation of the island. But it is graffiti that stands as perhaps the most disturbing reminder of Guam's history. Bus shelters, abandoned buildings, picnic shelters, fences, and in some villages the white-washed bases of memorials, are covered with commentary. Who should leave, who should stay. Words, many of them angry, remain perhaps the most powerful testament to what has been lost there. As Anne Michaels writes in her poem "What the Light Teaches," *Language remembers.*

June 08/98